O Come O Come Emmanuel

TO CELEBRATE JESUS' COMING WITH HOPE FOR ALL

John Cox

kevin mayhew

kevin mayhew

First published in Great Britain in 2016 by Kevin Mayhew Ltd
Buxhall, Stowmarket, Suffolk IP14 3BW
Tel: +44 (0) 1449 737978 Fax: +44 (0) 1449 737834
E-mail: info@kevinmayhew.com

www.kevinmayhew.com

9 8 7 6 5 4 3 2 1 0

ISBN 978 1 84867 848 4
Catalogue No. 1501522

Cover design by Rob Mortonson
© Image used under licence from Shutterstock Inc.
Edited by Nicki Copeland
Typeset by Angela Selfe

Printed and bound in Great Britain

Contents

About the author

Having spent rather a long time at various universities including Cambridge, Oxford and the University College of Rhodesia and Nyasaland, John was ordained to a curacy in the diocese of Liverpool in 1968. He spent a second curacy in an inner-city ex-slum parish in Birmingham and became rector in the same parish. After a five-year period at Church House, Westminster where he was Senior Selection Secretary, helping to select ordinands, he was made Canon Treasurer at Southwark Cathedral and Diocesan Director of Ordinands and Postordination training.

Following four years as Vicar of Roehampton he moved to become Archdeacon of Sudbury in the Diocese of St Edmundsbury and Ipswich in 1995. When he retired in 2006 he was asked to be the part-time Diocesan Director of Education, a job he did for nearly four and a half years before retiring for a second time. It has been during these retirement years that John has been writing for Kevin Mayhew, in between being chair of governors at a primary academy, playing golf and enjoying river cruises.

For details of all John Cox's books, please visit our website: www.kevinmayhew.com

Introduction

Advent is a time for looking forward – a time of expectation. We look forward to Christmas, to the coming of Jesus as a baby. But we look forward also to the coming of Jesus into our lives and into the life of the world. Traditionally we also look forward to the coming of Jesus again – his return in clouds of glory.

When I was a child, looking forward to Christmas was a delight and a pain. It was a delight because of all the pleasures it would bring – the family traditions of gathering together, of eating that special dinner, the decorations, and of course the presents. But it was also a pain – it took so long to arrive. 'O come, O come Emmanuel' we would sing. And what I wanted to sing was, 'O do come on' – get a move on. Childhood is not known for its patience.

Perhaps there is an element of impatience in all our longings for the presence of Christ to come as a reality in our lives, in the life of the Church, in the life of the world. It is not the impatience and longing of Israel of old looking for God to come in power to save and rescue. As Christians we believe that has already happened: in Jesus, God did come ('Emmanuel' means 'God with us'). His power was seen as loving sacrifice, his saving work as rescue for the whole world. We know Jesus came, and during Advent we prepare to celebrate that coming. The decisive act has already occurred, but its working out in the world and in the lives of individuals is a 'work in progress'. The kingdom has come, and we long for its coming. Our singing of 'O come, O come Emmanuel' is not just a repetition of a now fulfilled hope; it is still a real longing.

Advent

It is thought that originally Advent had no association with Christmas at all but was 40 days of preparation for those who were to be baptised in January at the feast of the Epiphany. During that Epiphany season not only was the visit of the wise men to the infant Jesus remembered (Matthew 2:1-12), but also Jesus' baptism in the Jordan (John 1:29-34) and his first miracle at the wedding at Cana (John 2:1-11). By the sixth century, Advent was associated with the coming of Christ – not as a baby in Bethlehem but his return on the clouds of glory. The practice of preparing for the celebration of Christ's birth with a period of fasting and abstinence, known as the Nativity fast, first occurred in the Middle Ages.

The length of Advent has varied over the centuries. Since the time of Pope Gregory VII (1073–85) it has been normal in the western Church for Advent to begin on the fourth Sunday before Christmas – the Sunday nearest to St Andrew's Day on 30 November. Previously there had been five weeks of preparation. Advent has also been celebrated for the seven weeks following St Martin's Day on 11 November until Christmas Eve, giving rise to the alternative name of St Martin's Lent. In the Celtic tradition and in the Orthodox Church, Advent begins on 15 November, offering a more obvious 40 days of fasting and in honour of St Philip whose feast day is 15 November. This period also has the name of St Philip's Lent.

In the Revised Common Lectionary, the readings for the four Sundays of Advent provide the following themes:

First Sunday: The Second Coming
Second Sunday: John the Baptist announces the coming of
                         the Messiah

Third Sunday: John the Baptist baptises Jesus
Fourth Sunday: Mary (the Annunciation and visit
                  to Elizabeth)

Wreaths and candles

It is suggested that the group might like to have its own Advent wreath, lighting a candle at each of the sessions to mark the weeks of Advent.

The lighting of a circle of candles during the long, dark winter months probably goes back to Norse times. The candles were set around a wheel that represented the earth, and prayers were offered to the god of light. They were used as a sign of hope for the return of the sun and the coming of spring. In the Christian tradition it is generally agreed that the use of a wreath with candles during the Advent season began with the Lutherans. It was part of the preparation for the coming of the one who is the Light of the world.

The wreath itself, made of evergreens, signifies life everlasting, while individual sprays have their own significance: laurel for victory over persecution; yew and pine for immortality, and cedar for strength and healing. The use of holly is especially associated with Christ's Passion since in some traditions the cross is said to have been made of holly, as was the crown of thorns. So together the wreath symbolises both death and suffering and healing and immortality.

The number of candles can vary – either four or five – as can their colour. The use of four candles indicates the four weeks of Advent and also represents the 4000 years that were thought to be the time between creation and the coming of Jesus. Sometimes a fifth candle, representing Christ, is added for use on Christmas Day itself. It is white. Three of the other candles are normally purple or blue, this being a penitential season, with the fourth being pink. The pink candle is traditionally lit on the third Sunday of Advent, known as Gaudete Sunday. The name comes from the first words of the Introit used at the Mass on that Sunday: 'Rejoice in the Lord always, and again I say rejoice' (Philippians 4:4). Being halfway through the season of abstinence and fasting, this was a Sunday of joy when there was a sense of relief from the austerities of the fast. This is comparable to the fourth Sunday in Lent when there is a relaxation of the demands of Lenten discipline. That is known as Laetare Sunday, from its Introit which begins with the words, 'Rejoice, O Jerusalem' (Isaiah 66:10). Its more common name is 'Refreshment Sunday'.

Churches vary in the meaning they give to each of the candles – for example, expectation, hope, joy and purity.

The candles are lit one by one on each of the Sundays, and prayers on the theme of the week are said as they are lit. The prayers given here are among those offered in *The Promise of his Glory*.[1]

First Sunday: The patriarchs

Blessed are you, Sovereign Lord, God of our ancestors;
to you be praise and glory for ever!
You called the patriarchs to live by the light of faith
and to journey in the hope of your promised fulfilment.
May we be obedient to your call
and be ready and watchful to receive your Christ,
a lamp to our feet and a light to our path;
for you are our light and our salvation.
Blessed be God for ever.

---

1. Church House Publishing, 1991.

Second Sunday: The prophets

Blessed are you, Sovereign Lord, just and true;
to you be praise and glory for ever!
Of old you spoke by the mouth of your prophets
but in our days you speak through your Son
whom you have appointed the heir of all things.
Grant us, your people, to walk in his light
that we may be found ready and watching
when he comes in glory and judgement;
for you are our light and our salvation.
Blessed be God for ever.

Third Sunday: John the Baptist

Blessed are you, Sovereign Lord, just and true;
to you be praise and glory for ever!
Your prophet John the Baptist was witness to the truth
as a burning and shining light.
May we your servants rejoice in his light,
and so be led to witness to him
who is the Lord of our coming Kingdom,
Jesus our Saviour and King of the ages.
Blessed be God for ever.

Fourth Sunday: The Virgin Mary

Blessed are you, Sovereign Lord, merciful and gentle;
to you be praise and glory for ever!
Your light has shone in our darkened world
through the child-bearing of blessed Mary;
grant that we who have seen your glory
may daily be renewed in your image
and prepared like her for the coming of your Son,
who is the Lord and Saviour of all.
Blessed be God for ever.

The Great Antiphons

The six sessions of this course are based on the verses of the hymn already referred to: 'O come, O come Emmanuel'. The hymn is deeply grounded in the tradition of the Church and has its roots way back in the sixth century. The hymn we sing today is a translation of a Latin hymn which reflected what is known as the Great Os of Advent. Since ancient times, the liturgy of the Church has included the singing of the Magnificat at the evening service of Vespers together with a response known as an Antiphon. The response is a verse from Scripture – usually, but not always, from the Psalms.

The Antiphons for the final week of Advent focus on the coming of the Messiah as a fulfilment of ancient prophecies. In the Middle Ages these particular Antiphons also echoed the verse used as the acclamation for the gospel during that week. They came to be known as 'The Great Antiphons' or 'The Great Os' because each verse began with the exclamation 'O'. Figures from the Old Testament: Wisdom, Ruler of Israel, Root of Jesse, Key of David, Rising Dawn, King of the Gentiles and Emmanuel are used as 'types' of the Messiah, the one to come: the Emmanuel. In their Latin form these were: *Sapienta, Adonai, Radix, Clavis, Oriens, Rex, Emmanuel.* Their initials made an acrostic which, read backwards, made 'Ero cras': 'Tomorrow I will be there.' This was understood to be a clear reference to the approaching Christmas vigil, although some scholars have suggested that this was all a matter of coincidence.

Sapienta

O Wisdom, coming forth from the mouth of the Most High,
reaching from one end to the other,
mightily and sweetly ordering all things:
Come and teach us the way of prudence.

Adonai

O Adonai, and leader of the House of Israel,
who appeared to Moses in the fire of the burning bush
and gave him the Law on Sinai:
Come and redeem us with an outstretched arm.

Radix

O Root of Jesse, standing as a sign among the peoples;
before you kings will shut their mouths,
to you the nations will make their prayer:
Come and deliver us, and delay no longer.

Clavis

O Key of David and sceptre of the House of Israel;
you open and no one can shut;
you shut and no one can open:
Come and lead the prisoners from the prison house,
those who dwell in darkness and the shadow of death.

Oriens

O Morning Star,
splendour of light eternal and sun of righteousness:
Come and enlighten those who dwell in darkness and the
shadow of death.

Rex

O King of the nations, and their desire,
the cornerstone making both one:
Come and save the human race,
which you fashioned from clay.

Emmanuel

O Emmanuel, our king and our lawgiver,
the hope of the nations and their Saviour:
Come and save us, O Lord our God.
(Translation from *Common Worship*)

A hymn reflecting the Great Antiphons may have existed as early as the eighth century, but clear proof of such a hymn dates from rather later in the twelfth century. It was in the nineteenth century that John Mason Neale's translation into English made the hymn more widely available, and it rapidly became popular. Although other translations have been produced, this is still the best known. However, with only five verses it does not include all the Antiphons: it omits Wisdom, and Emmanuel is part of the chorus.

Looking

Advent, like Lent, is an opportunity for us to pause and reflect. Amid all the bustle and busyness of the pre-Christmas period, finding time to withdraw from the rush and the anxiety is perhaps all the more important if we are to keep things in proportion. An Advent course, whether undertaken as part of a group or on one's own, provides the opportunity for a reality check – the reality of who we are and what our world is, the reality of our hopes as well as our fears. It encourages us to look afresh at the reality of the one who comes – how much is he really a part of our lives?

As we look forward this Advent, we will be encouraged to look in other directions as well – to look around at those who are lost and alienated, at outcasts and refugees;

to look inward at what is within us and within the world, especially in the darker parts; to look up to find hope and aspiration; to look with gratitude; and to look with the eyes of loving response as we meet with Christ, the one we long for, the one who we believe comes to meet the needs of our world and ourselves.

How to use this book

This short course is intended for use by small groups but could equally be helpful for individual use in setting a framework for private study, devotion and reflection. There are, however, advantages in using it in the context of joint study with others. There is not only the normal advantage of social interaction but also the stimulus of being able to draw upon one another's insights and experiences. To do so most fully requires a level of trust, because in some circumstances the discussion could lead to the sharing of quite private matters, both of faith and of a personal nature. No one should feel under any pressure to say more than they feel comfortable saying, and it would be advisable for a group to agree at an early stage how they wish to handle the issue of confidentiality.

Each session has a short reflection, and it will usually be helpful for the members of the group to have read this before attending the session. Some leaders fear that if this is encouraged, members will also pre-empt the discussion by looking at the session material and sorting out beforehand their answers to the questions offered. Frankly, I think this is more the leader's problem than anyone else's. Most people gain much more from discussion if they have had the opportunity to think about it in advance and to read something on the background of the points involved. Either way, it might be helpful to offer some time for the reflection to be looked at during the session itself, not least as a reminder of what it says. The whole point of the group meetings is to learn from the material and from each other – it's not a test! And that also means that if you feel you don't know a lot, don't worry. You're probably not the only one. What you do know is how you feel, what your experience has been, and what your faith (or even lack of it) means to you. And that is what is important. Being open to something new is more important than how much or how little you already know.

The sessions

What is offered here is a starting point, an outline, just one way of considering the material. The precise way each session is set out may not suit your particular group, so do feel free to use it flexibly. It's an aid, not a straitjacket.

It can be helpful to involve people in appropriate ways – for example, in the lighting of the candle in the Advent wreath, in reading, in leading the prayers. The offering of a place to meet could be one person's way of making a particular contribution. Churches or halls are not always the best or most comfortable places to meet, and a person's home can be both warm and welcoming. Whether refreshments are offered is very much up to the group. Some will enjoy having a meal together – so long as this doesn't become a cooking competition! For others, a cup of tea or coffee will be enough. This will also be dependent on the time members wish to give to the session. The discussion itself should normally last no more than about an hour and a half.

How the group considers the questions posed will be up to them. Some might find it helpful to start the discussion in pairs or threes and then open it up to the whole group. There is no prescribed pattern; just do what suits you.

Some groups will find a time of open prayer strange, and individuals may be reticent to offer prayers. In other groups, such opportunities to share concerns or delights in prayer may be very familiar. It is part of the leader's job to be sensitive to this, as to other things. Silence makes some people uneasy and there is a tendency to want to fill it. For others, it is a precious time of reflection and they are grateful that opportunities for prayer include silence.

Leaders

The time when it was thought that only the clergy could lead a study group has, hopefully, long disappeared. Whoever acts as leader, whether for the whole course or for just one session, should take time to prepare the session, reading through the material carefully and having some idea how the session should be shaped. This does not mean having such tight control that there is no room for interesting diversions, but it does mean having some idea about the timing of each section so that, for example, the prayers at the end are not rushed because time has run out. Sensible time-keeping is important.

It will be up to the leader to ensure that on the one hand no one person, including themselves, dominates the discussion, and that on the other hand all who have something to say are given an opportunity. Some members may be quite reticent and need a little encouraging. For some, being silent is far from implying they are not fully involved.

If the leader is not the host, then it will be important that there is some liaison between the leader and host to ensure that there is enough seating, when the refreshments (if any) should be offered, that the arrangements for the candles (if used) are appropriate and safe, and that any other required equipment, such as a CD player, is available (and working).

However careful the preparation, it is unlikely that the session will actually go precisely as planned. And that is fine, so long as it doesn't actually get entirely out of control. But it does mean that the leader will need to be aware of how the balance of the session is going and adapt it accordingly, for example by reducing the number of questions tackled.

There may well be differences of opinion expressed in the group and that can, occasionally, lead to quite heated discussion. The leader will need to handle this in a way that is sensitive to the openness of different views without allowing the argument to become personal. What is desirable is an atmosphere of trust where views are listened to carefully and with respect, and where difference is seen as a stimulus to discussion, not a matter for confrontation.

Music suggestions

Many groups find that having suitable music played, perhaps at the beginning as everyone settles down or during a time of reflection, can be helpful. In the sessions that follow I have merely suggested that there might be music at the end, but it is up to the group to do what feels best for them.

Here are some suggestions of CDs that are available from Kevin Mayhew:[2]

Margaret Rizza: *Icons* (Cat. No. 1490109)
Music for Reflective Prayer (3 CDs, Cat. No. 1490276)
Colin Mawby: *Be Still, My Soul* (Cat. No. 1490138)
Piano Music for Quiet Prayer (3 CDs, Cat. No. 3612282)

2. www.kevinmayhew.com.

Calming Classics (Cat. No. 1490226)
Serenity (Cat. No. 1490389)
Relax 1 (Cat. No. 1490314)
Relax 2 (Cat. No. 1490438)
Keep Calm and Reflect (Cat. No. 1490435)

Session One

God's welcome to all

The leader welcomes everyone. In preparation for the session the group is invited to sit quietly for a few minutes. Suitable music may be played, and the following verses may be used to help reflection.

Psalm 25:4-7

Make me to know your ways, O Lord;
teach me your paths.
Lead me in your truth, and teach me,
for you are the God of my salvation;
for you I wait all day long.

Be mindful of your mercy, O Lord, and of your steadfast love,
for they have been from of old.
Do not remember the sins of my youth or my transgressions;
according to your steadfast love remember me,
for your goodness' sake, O Lord!

Personal prayer

Come, Holy Spirit,
open my heart and mind to the wonders of your truth
and to the coming of our Lord, Emmanuel.
Through reading and reflection
may I hear the word of God speaking to me,
and know Christ is present with me,
as I prepare to celebrate his coming.
Amen

Group prayer

Come, Holy Spirit,
open our hearts and minds to the wonders of your truth
and to the coming of our Lord, Emmanuel.
By your grace
may we speak and listen with courtesy and patience,
that we may learn of you from one another
and know the presence of Christ among us.
Amen

Candle

The first of the Advent candles may be lit in the Advent wreath,
and the prayer said together.

The light of Christ shines a welcome to all:
to the outsider and the outcast,
to the different and the disliked,
to the migrant and the refugee.
May all be welcome in Christ's name.
Amen

Hymn

The first verse of the hymn is read together.

O come, O come Emmanuel,
and ransom captive Israel,
that mourns in lonely exile here,
until the Son of God appear.
Rejoice, rejoice!
Emmanuel shall come to thee, O Israel.

Reading

Isaiah 56:1-8
Thus says the Lord:
Maintain justice, and do what is right,
for soon my salvation will come,
and my deliverance be revealed.

Happy is the mortal who does this,
the one who holds it fast,
who keeps the sabbath, not profaning it,
and refrains from doing any evil.

Do not let the foreigner joined to the Lord say,
'The Lord will surely separate me from his people';
and do not let the eunuch say,
'I am just a dry tree.'
For thus says the Lord:
To the eunuchs who keep my sabbaths,
who choose the things that please me
and hold fast my covenant,
I will give, in my house and within my walls,
a monument and a name
better than sons and daughters;
I will give them an everlasting name
that shall not be cut off.

And the foreigners who join themselves to the Lord,
to minister to him, to love the name of the Lord,
and to be his servants,
all who keep the sabbath, and do not profane it,
and hold fast my covenant –
these I will bring to my holy mountain,

and make them joyful in my house of prayer;
their burnt-offerings and their sacrifices
will be accepted on my altar;
for my house shall be called a house of prayer
for all peoples.
Thus says the Lord God,
who gathers the outcasts of Israel,
I will gather others to them
besides those already gathered.

Romans 15:5-7
May the God of steadfastness and encouragement grant you to live in harmony with one another, in accordance with Christ Jesus, so that together you may with one voice glorify the God and Father of our Lord Jesus Christ.

Welcome one another, therefore, just as Christ has welcomed you, for the glory of God.

Reflection

The Jews never forgot their experiences of exile. It was engrained in their corporate memory as clearly as the Holocaust has been. It was not simply the trauma of being a conquered people. They had been taken by force from the land that had been promised to them, the land of God's people. They were torn from the place of God's presence among them in the Temple, and many must have wondered whether they would be able to find God and worship him in a strange land of other gods. Their God, it seemed, had deserted them. In a foreign country they had no rights; they were the outsiders. They had been dispossessed – of their home and country, of their Temple practices, of their place as citizens.

The prophets who were sent to them spoke of the people's past failures, their disobedience, their turning from God and their breaking of the agreement that had been made between God and his people: the covenant. They made clear that the disaster that had hit the people of Israel was not a matter of misfortune or of God's arbitrary action. It was righteous judgement.

But there was another side to the prophets' message – a vision of hope, of return, of new beginnings. This was not achieved by subversion or rebellion but through the gracious mercy of a God who had never given up on his people, had never forgotten his side of the agreement. God would come to them to rescue them. As in ancient times the Exodus had been God's saving act for his people, so too the return from exile and the restoration of his people was understood as God's action.

Exile and rescue (redemption) from it became symbolic images of the existential plight of the Jewish people and of their longed for hope in God's saving future action. They longed for the final Exodus, the final return from exile when the Lord would act to save them forever, would establish them as his people in peace in a new order. This hope spoke into Jewish spirituality and has been taken up into Christian spirituality, as Christians also see themselves as 'exiles' from the heavenly order that is their true home, their true land, their true citizenship.

Interwoven into this message of hope for the Jews was a thread of hope for all. It was not always taken notice of, not always remembered, not always lived by. It was not the main colour and texture of the tapestry of hope, but a slight and slender thread that subtly modifies what can sometimes be seen as a very specific and even exclusive concern for the fortunes of the people of Israel. There is this hope that others could be included in the 'good times ahead'. God's welcome would be extended. It was, as we see in the passage from Isaiah 56, still couched in terms that we might understand as 'Law obedience'. At face value it looks as if God's inclusion of foreigners and eunuchs was real but conditional upon their keeping the commandments. But even in those terms, this was a radical extension in the understanding of God's welcome.

The image of exile was taken up in the thinking of the early Church, not least by Paul. We need to think of this in the broadest terms. In the passage above from Paul's letter to the Romans he is concerned about the way members of the Church are treating those who have different opinions on issues of behaviour – in this case concerning eating habits. He is anxious that they do not exclude those who differ. He calls them to remember that what has brought them together is God's welcome, not the correctness or otherwise of their behaviour. He is reminding them of the radical nature of God's welcome.

This is even more obvious when Paul speaks of the barriers that appeared so fixed, the barriers of race and gender, free and slave, and which have been broken down by Christ: 'There is no longer Jew or Greek, there is no longer slave or free, there is no longer male and female; for all of you are one in Christ Jesus' (Galatians 3:28).

In his recent book on Paul, Rowan Williams demonstrates how Paul's thinking here is a radical rethinking of the dominant social structures of his time.[3] In Paul's world, everyone had a clearly defined place determined not only by their gender or race but equally by their status as a citizen or migrant,

---

3. Rowan Williams, *Meeting God in Paul* (SPCK, 2015).

free or slave. Society was so structured that each person knew their place and, apart from the very occasional exception, such as when slaves (with their owner's permission) bought their freedom, they stuck to it. Personal social interaction was constrained by this. Paul's understanding was that in the coming of Christ there was not simply a loosening of social constraints but also a radically new order. Being 'in Christ', being the new people of God, being citizens of God's kingdom was to be members of a totally new social order. Response to God's welcome to all manifested in Christ's coming, made you a new creature and also part of a new social pattern in which none of the old definitions held. One's identity was now determined entirely by being 'in Christ', not by being Jew or Gentile, male or female, slave or free. The old norms of 'insider' and 'outsider' no longer held. For Jews, this meant that not only were they welcomed 'home' from exile, but so were non-Jews.

It is sometimes possible for us to become so used to such passages from Paul that, like music in a lift, they become just part of the background and we forget how radical they are. Or we leave them in the pages of the Bible as truths for the readers of Paul's letters in his day but without seeing their implications for us today.

Let me put it in these terms: 'in Christ there is neither British nor Romanian, Pakistani nor Arab; there is neither deserving poor nor economic migrant; there is neither English taxpayer nor refugee; there is neither gay nor straight, cross-dresser or transgender; there is neither fundamentalist nor liberal, high church nor charismatic. Welcome one another, just as Christ has welcomed you.'

In God's kingdom, what we are is determined fully and wholly by whether or not we are 'in Christ' – nothing else.

His welcome is to all. It is that generous, that mind-blowing, that all-encompassing. And he calls us to extend that same welcome to others in our fellowship and in our mission.

The ideal is clear. The reality too often falls short. Internationally the Anglican Communion is torn by controversy, and there are occasions when far from being welcoming to members, delegates to conferences refuse to attend or walk out if those with opposing views attend. Although its General Synod voted for the consecration of women as bishops, there are still members who speak less with love than with disgust to those who took an opposing view. Anglicans do not have a monopoly on such division!

Locally churches are divided by attitudes towards the liturgy, the personality of the priest or minister, and who has charge of cupboards in the church hall. The declared welcome Christians should offer is too often compromised when particular people appear at the church door. Church members are among those who wish to restrict who enters the country and to limit the extent to which they are afforded the full right of citizens.

There are those in our church congregations who mourn that they do not feel at home but are exiles and outcasts, tolerated perhaps but not truly welcomed. Too many churches – but, of course, not all – have failed to live up to that radical new order Paul declares was inaugurated when the Son of God appeared, and which reflects the amazing welcome to all that God has declared.

Questions

1. How do you understand 'God's radical welcome'?

2. What do you understand it means to be 'in Christ'?

3. Who are the 'insiders' and the 'outsiders' in your church?

4. How are people welcomed into your church? Are there any who might feel less than welcomed?

5. In 2015, net migration into the UK was at a record high of 336,000, and 31,400 asylum seekers came to the UK in the same year. What is your reaction to these figures?

6. In 2015, 50 million people worldwide had to flee their homes. There were 126,000 refugees in the UK – i.e. less than about 0.25% of the total number of refugees. Approximately 31,400 people sought asylum in the UK in 2015. In Germany there were 166,800; in Sweden 81,300; in France 64,000 and in Italy 56,300.[4] Do these figures make you feel differently? If so, how?

7. What might your church do if there was an influx of migrants or refugees in your area?

8. How does your church handle differences of opinion and conflict?

9. What might you include in a welcome pack for a family from a foreign country who have recently arrived and come to your church?

Prayers

The group is encouraged to join in a time of open prayer, including prayers of intercession:

* for all who are 'exiled' – from their country or from their families and friends;

* for all refugees and immigrants and for those who seek to care for them;

* for those who feel alienated by the Church.

---

4. Figures from the International Organisation for Migration and the Red Cross.

Prayer of thanksgiving

We give thanks to you, our gracious God,
that you have welcomed us to be members of your people.
May the love of Christ and the presence of his Spirit
make us gracious and open in our welcome of others,
that together we may prepare for the coming of our Lord,
Emmanuel.
Amen

The Lord's Prayer

May the Lord bless us and keep us
and all for whom we pray,
this Advent-tide and for evermore.
Amen

The group remains in quietness as the Advent candle is
extinguished. Suitable music may be played.

Session Two

Freedom

The leader welcomes everyone. In preparation for the session the group is invited to sit quietly for a few minutes. Suitable music may be played, and the following verses may be used to help reflection.

Psalm 32:1-2
Happy are those whose transgression is forgiven,
whose sin is covered.
Happy are those to whom the LORD imputes no iniquity,
and in whose spirit there is no deceit.

Personal prayer

Come, Holy Spirit,
open my heart and mind to the wonders of your truth
and to the coming of our Lord, Emmanuel.
Through reading and reflection
may I hear the word of God speaking to me,
and know Christ is present with me,
as I prepare to celebrate his coming.
Amen

Group prayer

Come, Holy Spirit,
open our hearts and minds to the wonders of your truth
and to the coming of our Lord, Emmanuel.

By your grace
may we speak and listen with courtesy and patience,
that we may learn of you from one another
and know the presence of Christ among us.
Amen

Candle

The second of the Advent candles may be lit in the Advent
wreath alongside the first, and the prayer said together.

May the Light of Christ
shine into the dark places of our world,
our Church and our lives,
freeing us from the tyranny of wrong.
Grant us your freedom, good Lord,
to live as children of light.
Amen

Hymn

O come, thou Rod of Jesse, free
thine own from Satan's tyranny;
from depths of hell thy people save,
and give them vict'ry o'er the grave.
Rejoice, rejoice!
Emmanuel shall come to thee, O Israel.

Reading

Isaiah 11:1-5, 10

A shoot shall come out from the stock of Jesse,
and a branch shall grow out of his roots.

The spirit of the Lord shall rest on him,
the spirit of wisdom and understanding,
the spirit of counsel and might,
the spirit of knowledge and the fear of the Lord.
His delight shall be in the fear of the Lord.

He shall not judge by what his eyes see,
or decide by what his ears hear;
but with righteousness he shall judge the poor,
and decide with equity for the meek of the earth;
he shall strike the earth with the rod of his mouth,
and with the breath of his lips he shall kill the wicked.
Righteousness shall be the belt around his waist,
and faithfulness the belt around his loins.

. . . On that day the root of Jesse shall stand as a signal to the peoples; the nations shall inquire of him, and his dwelling shall be glorious.

Jeremiah 23:5

The days are surely coming, says the Lord, when I will raise up for David a righteous Branch, and he shall reign as king and deal wisely, and shall execute justice and righteousness in the land.

Galatians 4:8, 9; 5:13, 14

Formerly, when you did not know God, you were enslaved to beings that by nature are not gods. Now, however, that you have come to know God, or rather to be known by God, how can you turn back again to the weak and beggarly elemental spirits? How can you want to be enslaved to them again?

. . . For you were called to freedom, brothers and sisters; only do not use your freedom as an opportunity for self-indulgence, but through love become slaves to one another. For the whole law is summed up in a single commandment, 'You shall love your neighbour as yourself.'

Reflection

The first thing to note is that in the hymn we have 'Rod of Jesse' while the Isaiah passage mentions a branch growing out of the stump of Jesse's roots. 'Rod' actually means 'branch' or 'stem', and the stump is indicative that the tree is dead. The prophet is therefore giving a promise of hope. Just as God could bring a live shoot from a dead tree stump, so too God's promise to David that one of his descendants (his seed) would establish his throne for ever (2 Samuel 7:16) would be fulfilled, even though the line of kings that came from Jesse (David and his successors) died out. The hope of a king descended from David to lead the people of Israel was never forgotten (see Jeremiah 23:5), and the Branch is seen by many scholars as a Messianic title.

It was believed that this hope was realised in the coming of the Messiah. Matthew and Luke set out to prove this in their different genealogies of Jesus (Matthew 1:2-17; Luke 3:23-38), showing that Joseph could trace his ancestry back to David. Indeed, it was because of this, Luke tells us, that the family had to go to Bethlehem to be registered at the time of the census. Bethlehem was called the 'city of David' (Luke 2:4). Jesus as King was in the line of David, and he demonstrated the Spirit-given qualities Isaiah had set out in his prophecy.

In referring to Emmanuel as the Rod (branch) of Jesse, the hymn highlights the predominant feature of his action – to bring freedom.

To be a slave is to be a possession – not a person. Slavery has been a feature of human society for millennia. We can find it uncomfortable today to know that it was taken for granted in the Bible. People could fall into slavery in any number of ways: through conquest, through debt, or as a punishment, for example. A fellow Israelite could only be kept as a slave for six years, and when they were given their freedom, the owner was required to give the slave animals from the flock, grain and wine (Exodus 21:1-4; Deuteronomy 15:12-18). A foreign slave was a slave for life (Leviticus 25:44-46). Although slaves were the property of their owners and could be bought and sold, just like any other commodity, the owners could not treat them entirely as they liked. An owner could beat a slave, but if the slave's face was damaged the slave would be set free (Exodus 21:26, 27). Unless engaged to be married, a female slave could be raped with impunity (Leviticus 19:20-22). A slave was not required to work on the Sabbath (Exodus 20:10). How far all of these regulations were observed is uncertain.

Slavery still existed in Jesus' time, and Paul offered instructions as to how the slaves and masters who were members of a congregation should behave (Ephesians 6:5-9). It is important, however, to note just what Paul says. Both the service of the slave and the treatment of the slave were to be undertaken knowing that each of them, slave and master, had the same Master in heaven and that both slave and free would receive rewards from the same Lord for the good they did. Such mutuality was part of the radical new order of society Paul believed had been brought in by Christ.

In spite of the laws in this country and elsewhere, slavery still exists today. The Borgen Project offers the following statistics:[5]

1. An estimated 29.8 million people live in modern slavery today.

2. Slavery generates $32 billion for traffickers globally each year.

3. Approximately 78 per cent of victims are enslaved for labour; 22 per cent of victims are enslaved for sex.

4. 55 per cent of slavery victims are women and girls.

5. 26 per cent of slaves today are children under the age of 18.

6. Iceland, Ireland and the United Kingdom tied for the ranking of 160 in the 2013 Global Slavery Index. However, in spite of this ranking in the survey, these countries are not free from slavery. In the United Kingdom alone, there are estimated to be between 4,200 and 4,600 victims of slavery.

7. The country with the highest percentage of its population in slavery is Mauritania, with approximately 4 per cent of the total population enslaved. This amounts to roughly 140,000 to 160,000 people. Mauritania's total population is only 3.8 million.

Slavery provided the background for the longing for freedom and the promise held out in the coming of the Messiah. It is the context for St Paul's particular emphasis on the freedom to be found 'in Christ' – especially in the letter to the Galatians.

However, the hymn we are looking at is more concerned with another form of slavery – slavery through the tyranny

---

5. borgenproject.org (accessed 28 March 2016).

of Satan, as it puts it. The spiritual battle is understood to be against the evil one who holds humanity in his power, ultimately consigning them to the imprisonment of death and hell. On the cross and through the resurrection, Christ has won the victory over the evil one, and even though people still die, death does not have the final say.

The ongoing struggle against evil is all too evident, and popular devotion has focused this fight in the person of St George, who traditionally rescued a young woman from the power of a dragon. The symbolism is clear, and the figure of St George features frequently in both paintings and sculptures, one of the most dramatic of which is to be found in the cathedral church of St George in Stockholm.

At the personal level we may well have demons to struggle with – habits, addictions and traits which constrain, restrict and sometimes threaten to overpower us. We may call them our 'habitual sins', those things we know we do and which are wrong, but which we find so difficult to avoid. We look to the power of Christ to free us from them – especially those we fight against but secretly enjoy. We may seldom speak about them, if at all, and seek to keep them private even though a wise priest, minister or counsellor might well be able to help us – if only we would let them.

It is the social evils we see around us that can be particularly destructive. The evil of abuse (1 in 20 children in the UK is a victim of sexual abuse, according to the NSPCC[6]) and domestic violence (2.1 million people in England and Wales are victims of domestic abuse, according to SaveLives[7]), the spiral of evil that

---

6. www.nspcc.org.uk/preventing-abuse/child-abuse-and-neglect/child-sexual-abuse/ (accessed 28 March 2016).
7. http://safelives.org.uk/policy-evidence/about-domestic-abuse?gclid=CO-9j_PL28sCFU-wq0wodb6gEgQ (accessed 28 March 2016).

can imprison generation after generation, the evil of greed and malicious gossip, the evil of undermining another's worth, and the evil of ruthless disregard of others.

We rejoice that Emmanuel has indeed come to free us from all that holds us and others in what is destructive to the human spirit. Christ calls us to join him in the ongoing struggle, to seek with him to bring freedom to those ensnared and imprisoned spiritually, mentally and physically.

Questions

1. How might you draw upon the freeing power of Christ to bring freedom to those you see as held by the power of evil?

2. Are there any dangers in using the language of 'demons' and 'Satan' when considering personal and social evil?

3. As a church, do you have an active concern for those who are victims of abuse or violence? What might you do?

4. Having a concern for prisoners is sometimes seen as the typical soft romanticism of liberal idealists. How would you wish to rebut this?

5. What do you feel restrains or imprisons you – as individuals, as a church, as a community?

6. How do you understand the assertion that Christ has come and won the victory against evil, freeing us from its tyranny, while we still see so much evil around us?

7. What do you make of the fact that neither Jesus nor Paul appear to have condemned slavery?

Prayers

The group is encouraged to join in a time of open prayer, including prayers of intercession:

- for all who experience slavery in our world today – in forced labour and in the sex industry;

- for all who are in prison, for the victims of their crimes and for those who work in the prison service;

- for all who by their skill seek to help those who are imprisoned in addiction;

- for Christ's freeing power available to us all.

Prayer of thanksgiving
We give thanks to you, O Christ,
for your victory over all that imprisons the human spirit;
for the freedom of inner peace
and the freedom from social evils.
We give thanks to you, O Christ,
for all who in following you
have fought to bring freedom to slaves,
to release victims from the chains of guilt and despair
and to free the obsessive and the addicted.
We give thanks to you, our Emmanuel.
Amen

The Lord's Prayer

May the Lord bless us and keep us
and all for whom we pray,
this Advent-tide and for evermore.
Amen

The group remains in quietness as the Advent candles are extinguished. Suitable music may be played.

Session Three

Light in the darkness

The leader welcomes everyone. In preparation for the session, the group is invited to sit quietly for a few minutes. Suitable music may be played, and the following verses may be used to help reflection.

Psalm 103:1-3

Bless the Lord, O my soul,
and all that is within me,
bless his holy name.
Bless the Lord, O my soul,
and do not forget all his benefits –
who forgives all your iniquity,
who heals all your diseases.

Personal prayer

Come, Holy Spirit,
open my heart and mind to the wonders of your truth
and to the coming of our Lord, Emmanuel.
Through reading and reflection
may I hear the word of God speaking to me,
and know Christ is present with me,
as I prepare to celebrate his coming.
Amen

Group prayer

Come, Holy Spirit,
open our hearts and minds to the wonders of your truth
and to the coming of our Lord, Emmanuel.
By your grace
may we speak and listen with courtesy and patience,
that we may learn of you from one another
and know the presence of Christ among us.
Amen

Candle

The third of the Advent candles may be lit in the Advent wreath
alongside the first and second, and the prayer said together.

May the light of Christ
scatter the darkness that covers the joy of our lives:
the shadow of sin and guilt,
the shadow of pain and suffering,
the shadow of grief and despair.
Shine among us and within us
O Christ, our Emmanuel.
Amen

Hymn

O come, thou Dayspring, come and cheer
our spirits by thine advent here;
disperse the gloomy clouds of night
and death's dark shadows put to flight.
Rejoice, rejoice!
Emmanuel shall come to thee, O Israel.

Reading

Isaiah 60:1-3

Arise, shine; for your light has come,
and the glory of the Lord has risen upon you.
For darkness shall cover the earth,
and thick darkness the peoples;
but the Lord will arise upon you,
and his glory will appear over you.
Nations shall come to your light,
and kings to the brightness of your dawn.

Luke 1:78, 79

By the tender mercy of our God,
the dawn from on high will break upon us,
to give light to those who sit in darkness and in the shadow
of death,
to guide our feet into the way of peace.

John 1:6-9

There was a man sent from God, whose name was John. He came as a witness to testify to the light, so that all might believe through him. He himself was not the light, but he came to testify to the light. The true light, which enlightens everyone, was coming into the world.

Reflection

When John the Baptist was born, his father Zechariah was inspired to deliver a prophecy we now know as the Benedictus (Luke 1:67-79). As well as describing the role John would have, it tells of the saving activity of God both in the past and in the future. Into the world's darkness, God in his mercy would send light like the dawning sun dispelling the gloom of night. In John's terms, this is the promise of the coming of the Light of the world.

Although the general intent of the passage from Luke is clear, there is some difficulty about the precise meaning of the details. The original word in verse 78, translated here as 'dawn', speaks of 'arising', and this could equally refer to the morning star, the sun, or even the east (as in Matthew 2:2). Just to complicate (or enrich) it further, the word could also mean shoot or branch, which nicely picks up on another Messianic title, as we saw in session two (Jeremiah 23:5).

But light is the dominant theme of Advent, and we shall concentrate on that here.

Modern urban life is full of light, so much so that for stargazers it presents a real problem. They have to get away from the 'light pollution' in order to study the night sky properly. Children from our cities who stay in the countryside for the first time can find the lack of street lamps and brightly lit buildings a little scary. Even adults can be disconcerted by it. Walking through a ravine in the Sinai desert at night is quite unnerving. The darkness is tangible and certainly makes the traveller vulnerable. Little wonder therefore that ancient peoples used the contrast of dark and light so imaginatively in describing their anxiety about the problems of their lives, both individual and national, and their hopes for a better future. Light reveals what is there, it highlights the detail and the wonder of the world around us, it shows up what is wrong and dangerous. We speak of the light of truth, the light of knowledge, the light of experience.

The people of God had known splendid times, but they had also experienced many dark times – times of famine, of invasion and exile, of occupation. There were also the dark times of disobedience and turning from God to follow other deities.

We, too, have our dark shadows in our world and in our lives.

Zechariah spoke of the light that would guide our feet into the way of peace. Although it is now more than 70 years since we have known the direct effects of war in the UK, there has been armed conflict in other places throughout that time. The wars in Afghanistan, in Sudan, in Iraq and in Syria are but a few of the worst. Every day there are news reports on bombing and airstrikes, cities under siege, the plight of civilians, atrocities too dark to broadcast. For anyone who is sensitive to this – and surely there cannot be many who aren't – the toll of death and destruction is appalling. While politicians talk and appear to achieve so little, we can feel helpless. The shadows of war hang heavily over us even from a distance, and we pray and long for peace and for light to dispel the darkness.

But war is not the only shadow that hovers over us. In spite of all that can appear so good in our national life, we are constantly told of its failures – in the Health Service, in our schools, in community care, in mental health provision, in homes for the elderly, in housing, in manufacturing . . .The list goes on and on. There is a kind of cumulative effect of all this that can hang over us as a shadow of anxiety. And in our modern consumer society where so much emphasis is placed upon individual happiness and where there are decreasing levels of resilience with which to face dark times, our national spirit seems troubled. There is not inner peace.

We look also for the light that brings peace in our personal lives. Too many people suffer from a lack of self-confidence. They lack a sense of worth which gives them a maturity with which to view themselves and others. Increasing numbers of lives are darkened by anxiety and depression. These are the commonest forms of mental disorder in Britain, with between 4 and 10 per cent of the population experiencing depression in their lifetime.[8] Between 2003 and 2013, 18,220 people with mental health problems took their own lives.[9]

It would be too glib, and frankly damaging, to say, as I have heard said from the pulpit, that no one with Christ in their lives would be depressed. But what Christ can and does do is throw light upon our values, where we put our trust, how we seek to give meaning to our lives. Our society and the social norms around us encourage the belief, even subconsciously, that it is by the acquisition of possessions that we are to find our worth. The popular view of science leads us to see measurable fact as the only truth when what really matters is meaning. Christianity is increasingly felt to be irrelevant while many seek a spiritual dimension through the exotic, through fantasy and through the weird. For the Christian, the light of Christ is the light of truth which brings true peace and meaning into our lives. It is the light of self-giving love rather than acquisitive getting. It is concern for the other rather than an all-consuming self-concern. It is the invitation to draw on the grace and mercy and forgiveness of God which can help to dispel the dark of guilt and a false self-reliance. It is a love that draws people together, away from the darkness of isolation and loneliness.

For many, the greatest fear is of death itself – or perhaps even more, the fear of the process of dying. In our apparently enlightened times we are less realistic about facing death than ever before. As we live longer we become more susceptible to

8. Mental Health Foundation: www.mentalhealth.org.uk/statistics/mental-health-statistics-most-common-mental-health-problems (accessed 28 March 2016).
9. Mental Health Foundation: www.mentalhealth.org.uk/statistics/mental-health-statis-tics-suicide (accessed 28 March 2016).

the myriad ills of old age. Medical skills and knowledge keep us alive longer, but not necessarily alive better. In the light of Christ's resurrection and promises, death does not have to be the great enemy, the blackest of shadows. Grief does not have to be without hope.

The Advent message of the one who comes as God among us, who comes as light to dispel the shadows of night that can all too easily surround us, is a message for us and a message for us to take to others, a message to live by and to share.

Questions

1. What are the shadows that hover over you?

2. In what ways do you find that Christ brings light and peace into your life?

3. In what ways do those who suffer from mental health feature in your church prayers and action?

4. How does your church seek to help the lonely?

5. What do you believe could be done to enable young people to be more resilient?

6. Does your church have a programme of pastoral care for the bereaved? If not, how might one be established?

7. How might members of your congregation be encouraged to talk realistically about death?

8. What passage from Scripture have you found most 'enlightening'?

Prayers

The group is encouraged to join in a time of open prayer, including prayers of intercession:

- for those suffering from anxiety or depression and for those who seek to help them;

- for those who have lost family members through violence or suicide;

- for all who work in hospitals and in the community to care for the mentally ill;

- for the terminally sick and for the doctors, nurses and carers who look after them.

Prayer of thanksgiving

You, Lord Jesus,
are the light that has come into our world
to scatter the darkness that overshadows us.
We thank you for your presence among us,
and for the light of your truth and your love.
We thank you for the gift of your Holy Spirit
to guide us in the path that makes for peace.
We thank you for the gift of one another,
that we may grow as a community of light,
bringing your light to others,
helping those whose lives are troubled by their darkness.
Amen

The Lord's Prayer

May the Lord bless us and keep us
and all for whom we pray,
this Advent-tide and for evermore.
Amen

The group remains in quietness as the Advent candles are extinguished. Suitable music may be played.

Session Four

Key of David

The leader welcomes everyone. In preparation for the session the group is invited to sit quietly for a few minutes. Suitable music may be played, and the following verses may be used to help reflection.

Psalm 130:2, 3

Lord, hear my voice!
Let your ears be attentive
to the voice of my supplications!
If you, O Lord, should mark iniquities,
Lord, who could stand?

Personal prayer

Come, Holy Spirit,
open my heart and mind to the wonders of your truth
and to the coming of our Lord, Emmanuel.
Through reading and reflection
may I hear the word of God speaking to me,
and know Christ is present with me,
as I prepare to celebrate his coming.
Amen

Group prayer

Come, Holy Spirit,
open our hearts and minds to the wonders of your truth
and to the coming of our Lord, Emmanuel.
By your grace
may we speak and listen with courtesy and patience,
that we may learn of you from one another
and know the presence of Christ among us.
Amen

Candle

The fourth of the Advent candles may be lit in the Advent
wreath alongside the first, second and third, and the prayer
said together.

May the light of Christ
guide us in our spiritual pilgrimage,
keeping the vision of life with God before us,
looking always upwards.
Open the door to your presence
O Christ, our Emmanuel.
Amen

Hymn

O come, thou Key of David, come
and open wide our heav'nly home;
make safe the way that leads on high
and close the path to misery.
Rejoice, rejoice!
Emmanuel shall come to thee, O Israel.

Reading

Isaiah 22:20-22

On that day I will call my servant Eliakim son of Hilkiah, and will clothe him with your robe and bind your sash on him. I will commit your authority to his hand, and he shall be a father to the inhabitants of Jerusalem and to the house of Judah. I will place on his shoulder the key of the house of David; he shall open, and no one shall shut; he shall shut, and no one shall open.

Isaiah 9:6, 7

For a child has been born for us,
a son given to us;
authority rests upon his shoulders;
and he is named
Wonderful Counsellor, Mighty God,
Everlasting Father, Prince of Peace.
His authority shall grow continually,
and there shall be endless peace
for the throne of David and his kingdom.
He will establish and uphold it
with justice and with righteousness
from this time onwards and for evermore.
The zeal of the Lord of hosts will do this.

Revelation 3:7, 8a

And to the angel of the church in Philadelphia write:
These are the words of the holy one, the true one,
who has the key of David,
who opens and no one will shut,
who shuts and no one opens:
I know your works.

Reflection

In Isaiah 22 we read of two high officials in the royal household: Shebna and Eliakim. They were stewards, 'masters of the household'. A steward had considerable power, for among his responsibilities was to decide who should be allowed to enter the king's presence. He was, in this sense, the doorkeeper. Shebna, it appeared, had abused his position in some way, perhaps by having grand ideas above his station. This seems to be indicated by the reference to the tomb he had had carved out in the rocky heights on the western slopes of the Mount of Olives, where royalty would be buried. Isaiah tells him, with a cutting little insult, 'The Lord is about to hurl you away violently, my man.' On that day, Eliakim would replace him, suitably attired in the steward's robe and sash. He would be given the keys to the household and, as was the custom of the day, these would be worn on his shoulder.

The earliest keys come from ancient Babylon and Egypt. They were wooden and rather cumbersome. The Romans made smaller metal keys that were sometimes worn on fingers, not only to keep them handy but also as a sign of the person's wealth – it was large enough to require a security box! In a large household, keys would only be trusted to the highest official and were thus a sign of power and authority.

To have the key of David therefore meant that that person had control over the realm of David – the city of Jerusalem and the kingdom of Israel. Jesus was seen to be the fulfilment of the promise that the seed of David would rule over Israel forever. He was also seen as the fulfilment of Isaiah's prophecy about the one with ever-increasing authority on his shoulder, establishing peace for the throne of David. He was the 'Key of David'.

This symbol of the key as representing power and authority is also linked with Jesus in the letter to the church in Philadelphia in the book of Revelation where 'the holy one, the true one' has the key of David with the power to open a door that no one else can close and to close a door that no one else can then open. Our hymn tells us that this is the door to heaven, the door to the presence of God. According to Matthew, Jesus told Peter that he would give him the keys of the kingdom of heaven (Matthew 16:19). This has led to Peter being portrayed holding a set of keys and is why it is popularly said that he stands at the 'pearly gates' of heaven deciding who will or will not enter.

Keys, of course, can both open and lock doors. Christians naturally emphasise what Christ has done in opening the door to God's presence. This raises the question of whether it can also be 'locked', closed against anyone. So-called 'universalists' would insist that because God's love and mercy are eternal, the door is always open to everyone – all they have to do is walk through. Some people may choose not to, but ultimately God's loving invitation will persuade all. Taking a different point of view, others feel that only those who have put their trust in Jesus and in his saving work can be allowed into heaven, and they would quote Jesus' words recorded in John's Gospel: 'No one comes to the Father except through me' (John 14:6; see also John 3:16-21).

When heaven is mentioned we no doubt imagine that we all agree what that means – more or less. The details may vary, but the general idea is clear: heaven is where those who believe in Christ go when they die. They enter the presence of God, the way there having been opened by Christ. Just where heaven is we may not know, and while we may talk about 'up there', we know it isn't simply somewhere above the clouds.

The images of heaven depicting it as full of fluffy clouds with cherubs playing harps may still be around but are probably not taken very seriously these days. These are part of the sentimentalism that has grown around the notions of heaven which have little to do with a Christian understanding but rather have developed as a way of comforting the grieving and giving hope to the living.

The Christian hope is founded not on wishful thinking or optimism, nor even on what has been promised, but on what Christ has achieved. Our hope of heaven is based on his victory over death, because the division between God and us has been bridged, the door of access has been opened, and because Christ's resurrection means that a new order has begun. This is usually understood to mean that those who are 'in Christ' share in Christ's new resurrection life so that when we die we go to join him where there is no death and no mourning, but there is one endless light. We go with our identities intact.

That is what many understand by 'the resurrection of the body'. We are not simply subsumed into a sea of eternal being but, in Paul's words, are raised with a body of God's choosing – a spiritual body. We will all die, Paul asserts, but we will all be changed, and this mortal body will put on immortality (1 Corinthians 15). And that is what most Christians understand happens at the point of death as we are taken to heaven. This is what the prayers at funerals tell us; this is what so many of the hymns about death and resurrection and heaven portray. In seeking to console and offer hope to a grieving person, we will say, for example, 'Just remember he's in a better place, gone to join your mum.' And the picture we convey is of a loving couple happily reunited as man and wife in the heavenly place where God is.

Scholars like Tom Wright have set a huge question mark against so much of this traditional way of understanding heaven, not to undermine the Christian hope or the amazing achievement of Christ but to set it more firmly in what they believe to be the biblical teaching.

Tom Wright takes very seriously the line in the Lord's Prayer which says, 'thy kingdom come *on earth*, as it is in heaven'. For him, heaven is not the place we go to immediately when we die, but is part of that new order which has already been inaugurated on earth and which, in the fullness of God's time, will be fully realised in the new creation of both heaven and earth. 'With Easter,' he says, 'God's new creation is launched upon a surprised world, pointing ahead to the renewal, the redemption, the rebirth of the entire creation.'[10] When Jesus talks about the kingdom of heaven (as found in Matthew's Gospel), he is talking not about some future place but of the kingdom of God already becoming present on earth, and for which we are called to work in the power of Christ and his Spirit. This gives a particular significance to what we do here and now.

> Every act of love, every deed done in Christ and by the Spirit, every work of true creativity – every time justice is done, peace is made, families are healed, temptation is resisted, true freedom is sought and won ... this very earthly event takes its place within a long history of things which *implement* Jesus' own resurrection and *anticipate* the final new creation and act as signs of hope.[11]

---

10. Tom Wright, *Surprised by Hope* (SPCK, 2007), p.306.
11. Wright, *Surprised by Hope*, p.307.

It is Christ who has opened the way and enables us to walk in it.

At Advent we look forward not only to Christmas but also to the coming of the one who opened the way of hope and new life through his death and resurrection, and who calls us to join him in building the kingdom of God (of heaven) until that time when he comes to bring in the new heaven *and* the new earth, in which those who have died in Christ will have their rightful place.

Questions

1. What is the most significant hope that you have for yourself and for others?

2. How might you and your church open the door to new opportunities for those who feel their life chances are restricted?

3. How do you understand 'heaven'? In what ways is it a comforting concept?

4. What do you find most helpful in comforting a bereaved person?

5. How far do you find the approach of Tom Wright helpful?

6. What are the signs of 'the kingdom' that you look for in the life of the world and of the Church?

7. In what ways do you draw upon the power of Christ and his Spirit in following the way that leads to heaven?

8. How do you understand the second coming of Christ?

9. Is heaven open for all?

Prayers

The group is encouraged to join in a time of open prayer, including prayers of intercession:

- for those who have lost hope;

- for all who grieve, especially anyone known to the group;

- for all who minister to the dying and the bereaved – hospice staff, funeral directors, ministers, friends and counsellors;

- for all who work for the kingdom of God – for peace and justice, for compassion and healing.

Prayer of thanksgiving
We give thanks to Christ,
for all that he has achieved to bring us hope and new life,
for opening the way to the Father,
and defeating the power of death.
We give thanks to Christ,
for the gift of his Spirit
to guide us and strengthen us
in following the way of God's kingdom.
We give thanks for all who accompany us
on our journey of faith and hope.
We give thanks to Christ, God with us.
Amen

The Lord's Prayer

May the Lord bless us and keep us
and all for whom we pray,
this Advent-tide and for evermore.
Amen

The group remains in quietness as the Advent candles are extinguished. Suitable music may be played.

Session Five

Lord Almighty, the giver of the Law

The leader welcomes everyone. In preparation for the session the group is invited to sit quietly for a few minutes. Suitable music may be played, and the following verses may be used to help reflection.

Psalm 51:15-17

O Lord, open my lips,
and my mouth will declare your praise.
For you have no delight in sacrifice;
if I were to give a burnt-offering, you would not be pleased.
The sacrifice acceptable to God is a broken spirit;
a broken and contrite heart, O God, you will not despise.

Personal prayer

Come, Holy Spirit,
open my heart and mind to the wonders of your truth
and to the coming of our Lord, Emmanuel.
Through reading and reflection
may I hear the word of God speaking to me,
and know Christ is present with me,
as I prepare to celebrate his coming.
Amen

Group prayer

Come, Holy Spirit,
open our hearts and minds to the wonders of your truth
and to the coming of our Lord, Emmanuel.
By your grace
may we speak and listen with courtesy and patience,
that we may learn of you from one another
and know the presence of Christ among us.
Amen

Candle

All four of the Advent candles are lit, and the prayer is said
together.

Lord of all, in whose love we live,
guide us by the light of your word
and by the gift of your law,
that we may learn what is your will,
and respond with love and thankfulness.
Amen

Hymn

O come, O come, thou Lord of might,
who to thy tribes on Sinai's height
in ancient times didst give the Law,
in cloud and majesty and awe.
Rejoice, rejoice!
Emmanuel shall come to thee, O Israel.

Reading

Exodus 19:1-8

At the third new moon after the Israelites had gone out of the land of Egypt, on that very day, they came into the wilderness of Sinai. They had journeyed from Rephidim, entered the wilderness of Sinai, and camped in the wilderness; Israel camped there in front of the mountain. Then Moses went up to God; the Lord called to him from the mountain, saying, 'Thus you shall say to the house of Jacob, and tell the Israelites: You have seen what I did to the Egyptians, and how I bore you on eagles' wings and brought you to myself. Now therefore, if you obey my voice and keep my covenant, you shall be my treasured possession out of all the peoples. Indeed, the whole earth is mine, but you shall be for me a priestly kingdom and a holy nation. These are the words that you shall speak to the Israelites.'

So Moses came, summoned the elders of the people, and set before them all these words that the Lord had commanded him. The people all answered as one: 'Everything that the Lord has spoken we will do.' Moses reported the words of the people to the Lord.

Romans 3:21-31

But now, irrespective of law, the righteousness of God has been disclosed, and is attested by the law and the prophets, the righteousness of God through faith in Jesus Christ for all who believe. For there is no distinction, since all have sinned and fall short of the glory of God; they are now justified by his grace as a gift, through the redemption that is in Christ Jesus, whom God put forward as a sacrifice of atonement by his blood, effective through faith. He did this to show his righteousness, because in his divine forbearance he had passed over the sins previously committed; it was to prove at the present time that he himself is righteous and that he justifies the one who has faith in Jesus.

Then what becomes of boasting? It is excluded. By what law? By that of works? No, but by the law of faith. For we hold that a person is justified by faith apart from works prescribed by the law. Or is God the God of Jews only? Is he not the God of Gentiles also? Yes, of Gentiles also, since God is one; and he will justify the circumcised on the ground of faith and the uncircumcised through that same faith. Do we then overthrow the law by this faith? By no means! On the contrary, we uphold the law.

Reflection

It was to Abraham that God revealed himself as *El Shaddai* (Almighty God). Elsewhere, and more frequently, he is simply known as *Shaddai* (the Almighty). This epithet comes via the translators of the Greek Septuagint where they use the word *pantokrator* – 'the ruler of all'. Their assumption was that the word *Shaddai* was linked to the verb which meant 'to destroy or overpower'. Other possibilities link it to a word meaning 'to be strong', or to a Semitic word which would have meant 'the one who inhabits the mountain'. There are hints of this in our hymn which speaks of the Lord of might and of the giving of the Law to Moses on Mount Sinai. That mountains were understood to be places of divine revelation is common and appears in the New Testament, in the accounts of the transfiguration (Luke 9:28-36) and the ascension (Acts 1:6-12).

In a world where all peoples were religious and all had their own gods, it was important to be sure that the god being worshipped was the god who could do things and, when matters came to the crunch, that he was the most powerful. It was also important to know how to please the god. In the centuries before the Hebrews came to understand that Yahweh was in fact the only God, they affirmed that among all the gods he was their God and that he was the most powerful. This was experienced in terms of his bringing them fertility in their crops and herds or victory in war, in destroying their enemies, in bringing them out of slavery and giving them success in their invasion of the Promised Land. He was the mighty one, indeed the 'all mighty' one, the creator and ruler of all.

Power is commonly understood to be an essential characteristic of the Divine. A god who makes no difference, who can't achieve anything, is hardly a god worth putting your trust in. So there is nothing unusual about the God of Abraham being a God of power. But what is the distinctive nature of the power exercised by God, the Almighty? A selective reading of the Old Testament could encourage us to think of Yahweh as little more than a divine warlord beating up those he disapproved of. This God is then contrasted with the God who is Father of our Lord Jesus, God of love and forgiveness, mercy and compassion. Indeed, versions of this approach have led to a simplistic comparison between the Jewish and the Christian religions, with the implication that Christianity is superior. This way of seeing it is of course a travesty, but in subtle ways it can lie behind the arguments used by many Christians to explain how they understand the difference between the religion of the Old Testament and that of the New. Paul is cited as a supporter of this view, not least in the contrast that he is assumed to make between the God of Law and the God of grace.

It is always easy to caricature those we disagree with. The Jews, it is said, were given the Law so that by keeping the Law they could be saved. Only of course they couldn't, and the proliferation of laws didn't help. So they made sacrifices to appease their angry God. In time, God decided to step in and sent his Son to offer himself as a final sacrifice and to show that it is by faith and not by obedience to the Law that we are saved.

There is, of course, some degree of truth in this, but it is not the full story. God's relationship with the Hebrews came about through his choice to make them his people, not because they earned it. The agreement he made with them, the covenant, was not a negotiated contract but an invitation backed by a promise – I'll be your God and you'll be my people. The Law was not a precondition but a subsequent code to show the Israelites what sort of behaviour a people of this God, a people responding to this invitation, should follow. Because it is human nature to sin (to fail to meet the standards the Law set out and to fully respond to the love God shows), they failed. There was indeed a pattern of sacrifices that lasted until the destruction of the Temple in AD 70, and Jesus was seen as the 'final sacrifice', but the God of the Old Testament, who out of love for his people had made the agreement with them, was also seen to be a God of mercy and forgiveness (e.g. Psalm 25:4-7), more interested in the way people treated each other, more interested in how they responded to his love than in the number of their sacrifices (Psalm 51:15-17; Amos 5:21-24).

What Jesus came to show is that this God of mercy never gave up on his people but came to bring in himself a new order to their relationship. The Law, as far as Paul was concerned, was neither sufficient for salvation nor irrelevant.

He upheld the Law, but it was set in the new context that the coming of Jesus introduced. Jesus said he came to fulfil the Law, not to destroy it (Matthew 5:17). We should remember, too, that Jesus said, 'If you love me, you will keep my commandments' (John 14:15). He didn't say, 'I will only love you if you first keep my commandments.'

What was important, and what the coming of Jesus highlighted, was that the initiative is always with God, not with humanity. It was this that at their most legalistic the Jews had forgotten. The welcome, the invitation, the first move is always God's. We are invited to respond with trust and with obedience to the Law, which is summed up as, 'Love God and love your neighbour'. But our loving is always a response to the love God first shows us (1 John 4:19). It is in this love, this self-offering vulnerability, that God in Christ showed his true power and might.

Questions

1. What do you feel are the main differences between the Old and New Testaments?

2. God is sometimes described as omnipotent. How do you understand this? Can God do everything and anything?

3. In what ways, if any, would you say God is vulnerable?

4. Advent is a time of fasting and penitence. How is this reflected in your time of preparation for Christmas?

5. What do you understand to be positive about the Law?

6. What distinction would you want to draw between breaking the Law and sin?

7. How might love have a place in the world of politics, commerce or finance?

Prayers

The group is encouraged to join in a time of open prayer, including prayers of intercession:

- for God's ancient people the Jews;

- for the leaders of the nations and those who exercise power;

- for Church leaders;

- for all involved in the legal and justice system;

- for the humility to know it is God who saves and that it is by his grace we can offer lives that are obedient to the call to love.

Prayer of thanksgiving
We give thanks, Almighty God,
for all the love you have shown
in sending your Son to us.
We give thanks, most loving God,
for the gift of your Spirit,
guiding and enabling us
to live according to your will.
Amen

The Lord's Prayer

May the Lord bless us and keep us
and all for whom we pray,
this Advent-tide and for evermore.
Amen

The group remains in quietness as the Advent candles are extinguished. Suitable music may be played.

Session Six

Emmanuel, God with us

The leader welcomes everyone. In preparation for the session the group is invited to sit quietly for a few minutes. Suitable music may be played, and the following verses may be used to help reflection.

Psalm 70:4-6

Let all who seek you
rejoice and be glad in you.
Let those who love your salvation
say evermore, 'God is great!'
But I am poor and needy;
hasten to me, O God!
You are my help and my deliverer;
O Lord, do not delay!

Personal prayer

Come, Holy Spirit,
open my heart and mind to the wonders of your truth
and to the coming of our Lord, Emmanuel.
Through reading and reflection
may I hear the word of God speaking to me,
and know Christ is present with me,
as I prepare to celebrate his coming.
Amen

Group prayer

Come, Holy Spirit,
open our hearts and minds to the wonders of your truth
and to the coming of our Lord, Emmanuel.
By your grace
may we speak and listen with courtesy and patience,
that we may learn of you from one another
and know the presence of Christ among us.
Amen

Candle

All four of the Advent candles are lit, and the white candle
signifying the coming of Christ is lit in the middle of the
other four. The prayer is said together.

Come, O Christ, Light of the world,
shine with the brightness of your love
and fill our hearts with love for you.
Come, Son of Mary, Son of God,
God with us, our Emmanuel.
Amen

Hymn

O come, O come Emmanuel,
and ransom captive Israel,
that mourns in lonely exile here,
until the Son of God appear.
Rejoice, rejoice!
Emmanuel shall come to thee, O Israel.

O come, thou Rod of Jesse, free
thine own from Satan's tyranny;
from depths of hell thy people save,
and give them vict'ry o'er the grave.
Rejoice, rejoice!
Emmanuel shall come to thee, O Israel.

O come, thou Dayspring, come and cheer
our spirits by thine advent here;
disperse the gloomy clouds of night
and death's dark shadows put to flight.
Rejoice, rejoice!
Emmanuel shall come to thee, O Israel.

O come, thou Key of David, come
and open wide our heav'nly home;
make safe the way that leads on high
and close the path to misery.
Rejoice, rejoice!
Emmanuel shall come to thee, O Israel.

O come, O come, thou Lord of might,
who to thy tribes on Sinai's height
in ancient times didst give the Law,
in cloud and majesty and awe.
Rejoice, rejoice!
Emmanuel shall come to thee, O Israel.

Reading

Isaiah 7:14

Therefore the Lord himself will give you a sign. Look, the young woman is with child and shall bear a son, and shall name him Immanuel.

Isaiah 63:7-9

I will recount the gracious deeds of the Lord,
the praiseworthy acts of the Lord,
because of all that the Lord has done for us,
and the great favour to the house of Israel
that he has shown them according to his mercy,
according to the abundance of his steadfast love.
For he said, 'Surely they are my people,
children who will not deal falsely';
and he became their saviour
in all their distress.
It was no messenger or angel
but his presence that saved them;
in his love and in his pity he redeemed them;
he lifted them up and carried them all the days of old.

Matthew 1:18-23

Now the birth of Jesus the Messiah took place in this way. When his mother Mary had been engaged to Joseph, but before they lived together, she was found to be with child from the Holy Spirit. Her husband Joseph, being a righteous man and unwilling to expose her to public disgrace, planned to dismiss her quietly. But just when he had resolved to do this, an angel of the Lord appeared to him in a dream and said, 'Joseph, son of David, do not be afraid to take Mary as your wife, for the child conceived in her is from the Holy Spirit. She will bear a son, and you are to name him Jesus, for he will save his people from their sins.' All this took place to fulfil what had been spoken by the Lord through the prophet: 'Look, the virgin shall conceive and bear a son, and they shall name him Emmanuel', which means, 'God is with us.'

Reflection

The years immediately leading up to 732 BC were crucial in the life of Judah (see 2 Kings 16:1-20). Jerusalem was besieged by the Syrian army, assisted by forces from Israel, with the probable intention of forcing Judah into an alliance against the threat of Assyria. If king Ahaz failed to comply, the intention was to replace him with the son of Tabeal, a Syrian prince, who could be trusted to do as the Syrians wanted. Ahaz, fearful for his throne, was intent on an alliance with the Assyrians. Isaiah had warned him that such a policy would be disastrous and that the threat from Syria and Israel was negligible. Ahaz ignored Isaiah, who then invited him to ask for any sign he liked. Ahaz declined with a pious platitude. Nevertheless, a sign was given: a young woman in the court (possibly one of the king's wives) was pregnant and would give birth. The significant point was the child's name: he would be called 'Immanuel' – a name that would assure the king of the protection of God's presence (it means 'God with us'). Ahaz's rejection of this sign meant that the divine presence would work for disaster, not for rescue. This came about when Assyria invaded the northern kingdom of Israel, and Judah subsequently capitulated.

The passage from Isaiah 63 is part of a psalm, and these verses comprise what amount to a hymn-like confession of faith. It recalls the acts of God motivated by his 'steadfast love' (*hesed*), that attitude of God towards his people which led him to make the covenant with them, referred to in verse 8. The reference in the last verse is to the act of rescue in the Exodus where it is said (Exodus 23:20) that the Lord sent an angel to guard and guide his people. Here Isaiah is saying something even more daring – that God was with his people in person to save them and hold them. The psalm goes on to say what happened when the people rebelled and how the people longed for God to be with them again.

In quoting from Isaiah's prophecy, Matthew is telling his readers that the amazing new action of God is in line with God's intentions as revealed to the people of old, and is a fulfilment of it. The difference is that the presence of God now is not a 'spiritual' presence but is God seen in human form. The child is not simply the bearer of a name signifying God's presence; he is himself the bearer of God's presence. That all this is truly of God is made clear in the visit of the angel of the Lord – here to Joseph and, in Luke's Gospel, to Mary.

The strong love that God had shown in first making his covenant with the people of Israel is that same love that lies behind this culminating act of involvement with his creation. 'For God so loved the *world* that he gave his only Son, so that everyone who believes in him may not perish but may have eternal life' (John 3:16, my italics). That love was seen by John, as indeed it was in Matthew, with the story of the visit of the wise men, to be for all people, not just for the Jews. This is the start, as it were, of a new creation, a new covenant that extends to all people.

The passages we have been considering speak powerfully of the loving concern that God has for his people expressed in terms of his direct presence with them to protect and save. God is not forced, cajoled or browbeaten into this. It is his initiative motivated by love. But it looks for a response: it is not a 'take it or leave it' relationship. This is the risk God takes, for that response is not predetermined. We are not forced to love in response to God's love for us. The people of Israel were free to be obedient or to disobey, free to accept God's loving relationship or to reject it. And disobey and reject is what they did on frequent occasions. The coming of Emmanuel presents humanity with the same choice: to respond to God's loving presence with trust and love or to turn its back on God with us. And both acceptance and rejection carry their own particular consequences. That is why, amid the hope and promise of Advent, there is also the possibility of judgement. This is how John expresses it, and it has a very Advent feel to it:

> Indeed, God did not send the Son into the world to condemn the world, but in order that the world might be saved through him. Those who believe in him are not condemned; but those who do not believe are condemned already, because they have not believed in the name of the only Son of God. And this is the judgement, that the light has come into the world, and people loved darkness rather than light because their deeds were evil. For all who do evil hate the light and do not come to the light, so that their deeds may not be exposed. But those who do what is true come to the light, so that it may be clearly seen that their deeds have been done in God.
> *John 3:17-21*

As Christmas approaches there is an increasing air of celebration both in the life of the Church and, in its own way, in the secular world. The time waited for, looked for, anticipated with busyness and impatience, arrives; angels sing and the Christmas lights seek to reflect something of the glory of the occasion. But within a day the Church celebrates the death of the first martyr, and this is followed by recalling the death of the children killed on the orders of a tyrant who feared for his power because of the coming of Emmanuel. The family was forced to join the long trail of refugees that have fled for their safety throughout the centuries. The light came. God was indeed with us – and choices made in response to that were, as now, mixed and sometimes tragic in their consequences.

It is through this freedom to make choices that the possibility of making the wrong ones is always present. Wrong choices that go against what God wants for us and asks of us are sin. Life in Christ, guided and empowered by his Spirit, is what being truly human is all about. At best we strive for this, seeking to live more fully following the example of Christ.

For Jesus, too, there were always choices. His life was no more predetermined than our lives are. He was a Son, not a puppet dancing to the string-pulling of a puppet-master God. The choices Jesus made involved obedience to the Father but, in his God-given freedom, there was always the possibility of disobedience. Thankfully he made the right choices, even though it was at the greatest cost. The writer of the letter to the Hebrews puts it this way: 'In the days of his flesh, Jesus . . . although he was a Son, he learned obedience through what he suffered; and having been made perfect, he became the source of eternal salvation for all who obey him' (Hebrews 5:7-9).

The wonder of Christmas begins with the story of Emmanuel, but even the presence of God among us was not enough. The popular Christmas song, 'Mary's Boy Child', is wrong – it is *not* because of Christmas Day that we shall live for evermore, are saved, even though it would not have been possible without the birth of Christ. The negative response of men and women that has marred the relationship between God and his creation from the beginning means that the full extent of the need for Christ to come is not met simply by his presence but ultimately only by God giving himself away. And that is not the Christmas story; that is the story of Good Friday and, triumphantly, of Easter. In its own way, Advent is as much a preparation for that as it is for the Nativity.

Questions

1. It is said that God is all loving yet he also judges and punishes. How do you understand this?

2. How do you experience God's presence with you?

3. What signs do you see of God's loving presence in the world now?

4. In what ways do you understand God's judgement at work in the world and in the Church?

5. Christmas is more of a celebration these days than Easter. Why do you think this is so? Does it matter? What might Christians want to do about it?

6. It is sometimes said that, being divine, Jesus knew everything. In what ways do you understand the view that Jesus, even though divine, still had to learn?

7. What do you feel you have learnt this Advent – about God, about the world, about yourself?

Prayers

The group is encouraged to join in a time of open prayer, including prayers of intercession:

- for all mothers, especially those in labour and those who have recently given birth;

- for women who cannot have children and those whose babies miscarried or were stillborn;

- for families, especially those divided by war and by domestic violence;

- for the Church, that its Christmas celebrations may be joyful and welcoming to all, and proclaim the one who comes as God with us;

- for one another.

Prayer of thanksgiving

All praise and thanks to you, O God,
that in your love you sent your Son
to be born as one of us.

All praise and thanks to you, O Christ,
that in your love for us and for the Father
you remained obedient to his will.

All praise and thanks to you, O Holy Spirit,
that in your strength and by your grace
we may respond with trust and faith
to the love shown to us.
Amen

The Lord's Prayer

May the Lord bless us and keep us
and all for whom we pray,
this Advent-tide and for evermore.
Amen

The group remains in quietness as the Advent candles are extinguished. Suitable music may be played.